Benjamin Renner

Aus der Reihe: e-fellows.net stipendiaten-wissen

e-fellows.net (Hrsg.)

Band 918

Beyond the Corporation. Humanity Working by David Erdal - Book review

GRIN Verlag

Bibliografische Information der Deutschen Nationalbibliothek:

Die Deutsche Bibliothek verzeichnet diese Publikation in der Deutschen National-
bibliografie; detaillierte bibliografische Daten sind im Internet über http://dnb.d-
nb.de/ abrufbar.

Imprint:

Copyright © 2013 GRIN Verlag GmbH
Druck und Bindung: Books on Demand GmbH, Norderstedt Germany
ISBN: 978-3-656-64205-3

This book at GRIN:

http://www.grin.com/en/e-book/271875/beyond-the-corporation-humanity-working-
by-david-erdal-book-review

GRIN - Your knowledge has value

Der GRIN Verlag publiziert seit 1998 wissenschaftliche Arbeiten von Studenten, Hochschullehrern und anderen Akademikern als eBook und gedrucktes Buch. Die Verlagswebsite www.grin.com ist die ideale Plattform zur Veröffentlichung von Hausarbeiten, Abschlussarbeiten, wissenschaftlichen Aufsätzen, Dissertationen und Fachbüchern.

Visit us on the internet:

http://www.grin.com/

http://www.facebook.com/grincom

http://www.twitter.com/grin_com

Critical book review

Beyond the Corporation: Humanity Working by David Erdal, The Bodley Head, London, 2011. 320 pages.

In his most recent book 'Beyond the Corporation: Humanity working', David Erdal, book author and Non-Executive Director at Baxendale Ownership, strongly promotes the superiority of employee ownership. He gives a wide range of best practice examples across industries from various countries, without neglecting the essential theoretical foundation of the concept of democratic employee ownership. The book, which was published in March 2011, builds an argument around the financial collapse 2008 - 2009, when many traditional companies failed, suffered severely, or at the very least were shaken. David Erdal, who inherited Tullis Russell, a papermill business, in 1980s/1990s, which he eventually turned into a majority employee owned firm in 1994, illustrates how and why employee ownership leads to 'prosperity, health and happiness' (Erdal, 2011: 245). I have chosen 'Beyond the Corporation: Humanity working' for my critical book review for three reasons; the actuality of employee ownership particularly in Scotland (UK government, 2012), its publication in the aftermath of the recent financial crisis and Erdal's affiliation with the University of St Andrews as an Honorary Senior Research Fellow. However, while Erdal seeks to transform the flawed corporate status quo, which might appeal to most at first, his wishful thinking isn't a radical surprise (TEDxTalks, 2009), nor is employee ownership feasible for every enterprise (Hansmann, 1998).

The author elaborates employee ownership in four chapters. The first chapter exemplifies the unfavourable traditional work concept by outlining the unequal relationship between owners and employees in organizations. According to the author, they are far too often ruled by capital market discipline, and therefore prioritise short-term profits rather than re-investing, putting employee's jobs at a high risk. Even though there is a variety of forms for employee ownership such as direct (individual shareholders), indirect (employee trust), combinations of both, or weaker forms of employee involvement like control or earning rights only, the author desires direct employee ownership (Erdal, 2011 & TEDxTalks, 2009). He contrasts the prevailing corporate economy with the stories of four pioneers in the field of employee ownership – the Catholic priest José María Arizmendiarieta from Spain, the British John Spedan Lewis, Giusepe Bucci from Italy, Ernst Abbe who founded the Carl-Zeiss-Stiftung in Germany and the political economist Louis Kelso, who is regarded as being the originator of the Employee Stock Ownership Plan (ESOP).

Furthermore, he uses his own example of Tullis Russel to counter the arguments against employee-ownership of economists and businessmen alike regarding innovation capacity, growth and decision making. Subsequently, he goes back to the 18th - 19th century and describes the genesis of modern employment laws, power and the employment contract which he regards as 'incapable of reaching the heights of flexibility, innovation and productivity that are possible in a sharing model' (Erdal, 2011: 136). The third chapter is devoted to ordinary people that work for firms such as John Lewis, an employee-owned department store chain, who Erdal interviewed about their contribution and participation in business. Moreover, he speaks about the 'ownership effect' and concludes that 'working this way appeals to people at a deeply natural level' (Erdal, 2011: 172). However, he admits, a sustainable employee-ownership concept requires a workable, well-structured takeover (typically business succession) and exit process (funding, repurchase liability of the firm) and ultimately good governance (a culture of involvement of all owner-employees) to 'let humanity work' (Erdal, 2011: 223). If Erdal hasn't won you over by this point, his departure in the final chapter of 'Beyond the Corporation: Humanity Working' to times where humans were living in caves is unlikely to persuade you any further to abolish the prevailing shareholder-capitalism.

Erdal (2011) argues that the separation of workers and owners in enterprises needs to be abolished after two centuries of prevalence. Instead, he argues that they should be replaced by a relationship that is characterized by democratic partnership and supported by strong leadership, as this will eventually lead to higher productivity and satisfaction of employee-owners. He supports this by referring to 'available information' (Erdal 2011: X) without giving the precise details or any statistical data in the beginning. In fact, there are several examples of profitable employee-owned enterprises, particularly in the United Kingdom and United States (ESOP-A, 2013), as well as recent research supporting the thesis of higher levels of wellbeing (McQuaid, R., Hollywood, E. & Bond S., 2012). Erdal (2011) subsequently develops his thesis by emphasizing the importance of empowerment and information, the necessity of real ownership (leading to low absenteeism), a decrease in labour turnover and wealthier employees in terms of health and money. These arguments are supported by institutions such as ESOP-A (2013), in large parts by McQuaid et. al.'s (2012) research on behalf of the Employee Ownership Associated from London, and partly also by his own findings after having compared public data in Imola, Faenza and Sassuolo. Interestingly those points are not reflected in Levins' (1999) summary of possible advantages of employee involvement.

However, I think it is highly disputable whether these advantages are the decisive factor for reaching the 'healthiest possible economy' (Erdal, 2011: 6). To challenge this, I'd like to take the example of the German Mittelstand. German Mittelstand accounts for almost all German companies, the vast majority of these firms relying on their own equity or bank loans and with a long-term business strategy. It is widely renowned as 'Europe's economic driving force' (BMWi, 2013: 2). These companies are mostly family-owned, highly innovative and seem to have found a solid balance between governance and power, despite their traditional owner-employee relationships. My view is somewhat supported by Jensen and Meckling who declare that the traditional company has 'far survived the market test against potential alternatives' (Jensen & Meckling, 1976: 357). Hansmann also partly negates the importance of productivity and employee satisfaction. He puts at a question whether 'survival is a reasonable test of the efficiency of employee-ownership' (Hansmann, 1998: 47). The importance of employee satisfaction is far from negligible, however, it can be achieved without changing the ownership structure of the firm, by establishing a transparency across all levels of hierarchy and councils with worker representatives and by making work more exciting. All public companies in Germany, for instance, must have employees represented in their *Aufsichtsrat* (supervisory board), who appoint or relieve the *Vorstand* (management board), according to German law (Germany *Aktiengesetz 2013*). This example is also given by Hansmann (1998). This might be a suitable solution for other countries or even SMEs.

Specifically, Erdal (2011) criticizes the apparent prejudices against employee-ownership, namely slow decision-making, the lack of competitiveness (i.e. slow growth, resistance to change and reinvestment) and affronts the economists of our time who 'are no better at predicting the behaviour of employee-owned companies, than they are at forecasting the behaviour of bankers' (Erdal, 2011: 45). It appears that Erdal (2011) is too general in his arguments since he denies almost every single argument against employee-ownership. He repeatedly builds on the benefits for employees and a good organisational structure, which would, once established, offset possible weaknesses. He might win some readers over because he uses subtle, cleverly incorporated statements in the form of voices of other people working in large employee-owned companies like Mondragon or John Lewis Partnership. Fast decision-making processes are vital for companies that operate in a complex, fast moving business environment and for which innovation is key (i.e. pharmaceutical/chemical industry). I think fast and critical decision-making is hard to achieve for firms with a democratic employee-ownership structure, particularly in large enterprises with piles of information. Since more companies 'go global' and boundaries become indistinct in many regions, the personnel structure can be very diverse in regard to gender, ethnicity or race. It has even become a critical success factor for growth, the business strategy, or the corporate culture of many corporations, as recently shown by Ahern and Clarke (2013). My view on the importance of quickly passing corporate resolutions is generally supported by Levine (1999) or Hansmann (1998), who emphasizes even more the 'costs of collective decision-making' (Erdal, 2011: 46) occurring in employee-owned firms.

Even though Erdal (2011) makes an effort to convince the reader that difficult decisions are still possible by telling the success story of Tullis Russel, or giving employee-owners a voice, I miss sufficient empirical evidence. This remains an issue despite the author admitting that his 'book is mainly about arguments, illustrated with accounts of individual experience' (Erdal, 2011: X). Moreover, I am convinced that the excitement for labor-managed firms will not prevail once it is established everywhere.

While Erdal (2011) presents different models of employee ownership, he also raises the challenge of business succession or withdrawal. Nowadays, people in developed economies change their jobs more frequently than a number of years ago (OECD, 2013). Many ambitious employees want to create an impact, want to be listened to or included in business decisions. This means, under the assumption of wide-spread employee-ownership, companies have to pay their employees off, which might, depending on the amount of shares held by each individual and the size of the company, put an additional financial burden on it. I think it is unlikely that people can or want to (re-)invest in several businesses throughout their working life, since the money is tied up (unless employee-ownership would reverse the current trend of job hopping). I doubt the self-evident 'commitment of the people as human beings' (2011, 210), which Erdal uses to explain why people would want the company to re-invest their proportion of the profits. After all, the author wants employees to become wealthier while being shareholders of the companies to which they commit themselves every day, because usually shareholders are profit-orientated and from outside the organizational framework, devoid of emotional affiliation. Moreover, he criticizes the cruelty of capital market discipline and the maximization of shareholder value, which eventually encourages leaders to exercise their power and act morally reprehensible (paying themselves excessive salaries, immediately punishing bad employee performance instead of continuous improvement). According to Erdal (2009, 2011), sharing systems were proven to be 'the economically efficient solution' (2011, 237) during the Stone Age and are more than ever an attractive way to achieve a more uniform distribution of wealth. Certainly, the gap between rich and poor is widening, which is alarming. Employee-ownership may well make employees more prosperous if the company reaps profits, however, on a global scale, the extremely poor are living in developing countries, are refugees, uneducated or unemployed people (UN, 2013:6-17). Besides, not every employee might be willing to take the risk of ownership because some people are risk averse, even though a recent study by Bova, Kolev, Thomas and Zhang (2012) claims that an equity-based compensation for non-executive employees reduces the risk-taking behaviour of the corporation. Nevertheless, I agree with Erdal that a *'pas trop gouverner'*-policy in our imperfect markets doesn't sufficiently sanction short-term profit-making.

Overall, Erdal's 'Beyond the corporation: Humanity working' is an appealing book about employee-ownership, especially in view of the collapse of flagship companies during the financial crisis. The book, with its peculiar structure, is still easy to understand and a great introduction to this topic. To some extent, this is also because of the author's personal deep belief, his professional expertise and his credibility due to the role model function of his former business Tullis Russel and the supporting interviews. In contrast to earlier publications on employee-ownership, I miss the absence of brand-new, challenging input and the partly biased presentation of his arguments. Personally, I don't see the absolute necessity for a transformation process towards employee-ownership like Erdal (2011) and its practicality for global and diverse companies in a dynamic environment. I would rather see necessary improvements in regard to the empowerment of workers. Nevertheless, the book is an inspiring read for anyone from politics or academia who has not yet considered employee-ownership.

Reference list

Ahern, D. & Clarke, B. (2013) *Listed Companies' Engagement with Diversity: A Multi-Jurisdictional Study of Annual Report Disclosures.* Dublin: Department of Jobs, Enterprise and Innovation, Trinity College Dublin.

Bova, F., Kolev K., Thomas, J. & Zhang, F. (2013) *'Non-Executive Employee Ownership and Corporate Risk-Taking'.* Yale School of Management. Working Paper: 2013, May 21.

BMWi, (2013, July 1) 'German Mittelstand: Engine of the German economy' *(Federal Ministry of Economics and Technology, Federal Republic of Germany),* Available: http://www.bmwi.de/English/Redaktion/Pdf/factbook-german-mittelstand,property=pdf,berei ch=bmwi2012,sprache=en,rwb=true.pdf (Accessed: 2013, September 27).

Erdal, D. (2011) *Beyond the Corporation: Humanity Working.* London: The Bodley Head.

ESOP-A, (2013, September 10) 'ESOP Companies Report Economic Growth in 2012'. *(The ESOP Association),* Available: http://www.esopassociation.org/news-landing/2013/09/10/ esop-companies-report-economic-growth-in-2012 (Accessed: 2013, September 27).

Germany. *Aktiengesetz. Chapter 2.* (2013) Mannheim: Juristischer Informationsdienst.

Hansmann, H. B. (1998) 'Employee ownership of firms'. In P. Newman (ed.) *The New Palgrave Dictionary of Economics and the Law:* 43-47. London: Palgrave Macmillan.

Jensen, M.C., Meckling, W.H. (1976) 'Agency costs and the theory of the firm'. *Journal of Financial Economics,* 3 (4):305-360.

Levine, D.I. (1999, January 27) 'How Business and Employees Can Both Win: Advantages and Disadvantages of Employee Involvement' *(COHRE, Institute of Industrial Relations, University of Berkeley),* available: http://www.irle.berkeley.edu/cohre/levine/adv.html (Accessed: 2013, September 27).

McQuaid, R., Hollywood, E. & Bond S. (2012) *Health and wellbeing of employees in employee owned businesses. Final Report to Employee Ownership Association.* Edinburgh: Employment Research Institute, Edinburgh Napier University.

OECD, (2013) 'OECD Employment and Labour Market Statistics'. *(Organisation for Economic Co-operation and Development iLibrary),* Available: http://stats.oecd.org/ BrandedView.aspx?oecd_bv_id=lfs-data-en&doi=lfs-lfs-data-en (Accessed: 2013, October 04).

UK government, (2012, July 4) 'Sharing success: The Nuttall Review of Employee Ownership'. *(UK government publications),* Available: https://www.gov.uk/government/ uploads/system/uploads/attachment_data/file/31706/12-933-sharing-success-nuttall-review-employee-ownership.pdf (Accessed: 2013, September 27).

UN, (2013, July 1) 'The Millennium Development Goals Report'. *(United Nations New York),* Available: http://www.un.org/millenniumgoals/pdf/report-2013/mdg-report-2013-english.pdf (Accessed: 2013, September 23).

TEDxTalks. (2009) *TEDxEdinburgh - David Erdal - 11/26/09* [Video] Available from: http://www.youtube.com/watch?gl=GB&v=yO3WaCvxbbg (Accessed: 2013, September 29).